I0143410

FROM

GRIEVING TO

GRATEFUL

Written By

Shirley Stokes Jefferies

Copyright © 2017 Shirley Stokes Jeffries

All rights reserved. Except as permitted under the U.S.
Copyright Act of 1976, no part of this publication may be
reproduced, distributed, or transmitted in any form or by
any means, or stored in a database or retrieval system,
without the prior written permission of the publisher.

One11 Publishing
872 S Milwaukee Ave, Ste 195
Libertyville, IL 60048

www.one11publishing.com

Publisher: Sedrik Newbern
Editor: Antonio Mitchell
Cover Designer: Scott Ventura

Printed in the United States of America
First Edition: November 2017

Author's Note
This book is based on my life experiences for learning and
teaching purposes only.

ISBN Paperback 978-0-9982892-8-1

One11 Publishing is an imprint of
Newbern Consulting Group, LLC.

Dedication

This book is dedicated to my amazing
daughter, Raashad, my angel. You may be
gone physically but you will forever live in
my heart and the hearts of your family
who love you so much.

Contents

Contents

Acknowledgements

I would like to thank and acknowledge the Creator for all his Grace and Mercy.

Thank you to my children, Destiny, Damian, Jonas, Raashad, Jonathan, and Sharmelle. I love you all and thank God for each of you. To my little niece, Kievayana Joseph, who helped me correct my bad handwriting, I would not have been able to start this project without you. And thanks to the entire Stokes family. You all are always there for me. Thank you!

A very special thank you to my greatest inspiration, my Pastor Prez Jackson. He pushes me every time I think I can't go on. Also thank you to the entire Pleasant Grove Church family, whom I truly Love.

I also have to thank the team at One11 Publishing for your guidance, patience, support and creativity. You were able to bring my dream to life, so it can be shared with the world. I appreciate all you've done to make this book happen.

Lastly, I thank myself, because I have found that I am stronger than I have ever known.

So please, sit back, open your heart and minds and enjoy the book of poetry I call *From Grieving to Grateful.*

Introduction

It all began in the year 2000. Coming down from a jovial and joyous New Year's celebration leaving one century and entering into a whole new era. I made the statement "2000 is going to be 'my' year!" As luck would have it, it certainly was. A year filled with so much heartache and grief, it almost overwhelmed me.

It started in February of 2000. My father, who was normally a very active and outgoing 83 year old, began to feel as he described, "different." He went to the doctor, later to the hospital and within days pronounced dead. My dad was gone? No this couldn't be true. My heart took a nose dive.

As I said before, that was only the beginning. It seems death started coming and refused to take a break. Death came several times. It took uncles, aunts, close cousins and life-time friends. Then it came closer.

In September of 2000, death took my brother Roy. At this point, I'm literally reeling with pain and physically drained from death.

In November of the same year, my family and I decided we would celebrate my son's birthday when a sudden knock at the door led us to find death came by again. This time it was my mother. I just knew my life was over. Then in February of 2001, my sister, Christine, left to be with the Lord.

Death subsided for a while, but it returned and came back with vengeance on December 23, 2013. Preparing for the celebration of the birth of Christ, we had to stop everything and prepare for the home going of my daughter Raashad. This time death hit real hard. It broke me down as far as any parent can go.

I cried out, "God, please no more!" I wanted to question God and ask, "Why? Why her? Why my child?" I didn't, but God... he knows me better than I know myself. I had the audacity to even think I should or could question him. "No!"

Each time my family and I dealt with death and all the tribulations and pain it brings, our Pastor Prez Jackson, was right there to lift us and give us a word from God. One scripture in particular that stuck with me, God said in Isaiah 41:13, "For the Lord thy God will hold thy right hand. Fear not, I will help thee." That's the God we serve. In our darkest hours, He is ever present. And in that scripture, He let us know not only is He there, but He will help us. Oh Hallelujah to His name! Therefore I'm grateful.

Going through so much grief taught me several things that I still live by today... what doesn't kill me will make me stronger. Grieving can last a long time, but God's grace and mercy last longer. Thus, I shall continue to praise Him for He is good. To sum it up, God is Everlasting! In my darkest hours, I learned to be grateful. God gets all the glory!

My prayer for those reading my book of poetry is that you will see and feel my pain, but also see the glory my God has for us all if we would only just believe and trust in Him.

Memories of Mom

One day as I walking, not fast,
not slow, just thinking.
My mind and heart slowly started sinking
to remember you from days gone by.
I had to stop as tears came from my eyes.
I thought to myself these very words,
God won't take us to it unless
He brings us through it.
A merciful, powerful,
mighty hand passed my way
and said, "Fear not my child.
This pain won't stay."
I looked towards Heaven
from which all my blessings flow.
I shouted loudly and cried,
"I can't take this no more."
A voice responded quietly yet still,
"What I have done was only in my will."

Let not your heart be troubled,

and peace be still.

I know what I'm going through

is only a test,

'cause what God does for me

is only for my best.

You Gave Me Your All

Sometimes in life we never realize.

We never even stop or open our eyes

to see just how precious,

how dear, how true

someone in your life is

until their time is due.

But for you mom, the memories linger still.

How you'd do anything for me

at random or at will.

You gave life to me, wisdom,

knowledge, and care.

I never will forget you were always there.

In elementary you taught me my ABC's.

In Junior High the birds and the bees.

When I moved on and went to High School,

you taught me abstinence was still cool.

When I graduated you taught me more

aspects of life.

To take the punches with fear and strife.

To always love the Lord and do my best.

For this Mom, I'm certainly

trying to pass the test.

Truly my heart will grieve you,

because I'll never find anyone

to take the place of you.

So to God be the glory and

praises to His name.

For the love in my heart for you

will forever be the same.

Mom & Dad

How can we say goodbye
to our baby we loved so much?
We are gonna miss everything about you,
especially your loving touch.
You had a way to make us smile, even
when we felt so sad and blue.
We look to the skies and ask of Him what
will we do without you.

He whispers back and says to us, "She's
gone but not far away.
If you live right and seek my faith, you will
see her again someday."
Oh baby, we'll cry for you. Our hearts will
hurt. We don't know how long.
But when it comes to raising your babies,
we will be very strong.
Before you left that was your request,
to leave them with someone
who will love them best.
We will love them, because we loved you.
Our love for them will represent
the love we had for you.
God has retrieved
what belonged to Him first.
This is one day for which
we never rehearsed.
But we will do our best
to go on without you for now.

We know if we live right,

we'll see you again somehow.

In life, we loved you much,

and in death we love you still.

We know for you to leave us

was only God's great will.

A Poem For Mom

When I think of you

leaving me mom,

I want to scream

real loud.

'Cause my whole life,

I just wanted

to make you proud.

My biggest joy was

seeing you smile each day.

To get me through this, I gotta pray.

For this I know, God makes no mistakes

His promises, He keeps. The ones He love

He never forsakes.

This came to me all out of the blue.

My faith was shaken and tested true.

'Cause only God knows how much I love you.

Silent moments will bring a scream.

I hope I'll awake and this will be a dream.

But if it is reality, and this is all true,

I know if I live right, in heaven I'll see you.

You Taught Me

Dad you know I'm gonna miss you.
You were always there for me
to share some laughs, to talk about life.
How things could go wrong
and cause you great strife.
You showed me how to hunt,
fish and provide for myself.
To get the things I needed in life
and acquire some type of wealth.
Sometimes your lessons were hard,
I thought they were too tough.
But now as I reminisce,
they weren't tough enough.
You taught me that what won't kill
me will only make me stronger.
That lesson was taught when
I was much younger
Hindsight is always 20/20

and experience teaches us best.

Dad we will truly miss you.

Yet we know that God knows what is best.

So go on home dad and take your rest.

POPS

P is for **Preparing** me for life's
this and that's.
O is for **Owning** up to
the fact nobody is perfect.
P is **Putting** your life on hold
to make sure mine was straight.
S is for **Showing** me that
all works of God are great.
I'm gonna miss you Pops in a major way.
But how happy and rejoiceful
I'll be on judgement day.
God knows sometimes
we were like night and day.
But you always had my back.
You never walked away.
One day when I become a father
and I know one day I will be.
I hope I'm the friend to him
like you were to me.

Goodbye Dad

Dad, how can I say goodbye to someone
who meant so much to me?
To see you on this side with your health
failing you was so hard.
I never knew how to expect it.
I just played the part.
I tried to stand up
and be a man for my mother.

To endure the pain

like my sisters and brothers.

But it's been hard for a while now Dad.

Sometimes just seeing you

would make me sad.

I was use to a strong, energetic man,

who was always in good spirits

and good health.

Never caring about riches

or having lots of wealth.

Just living day by day

doing the best you could.

Doing for others

what you thought was good.

Teaching my brothers and I about the

challenges of manhood.

Dad, you know we will miss you.

Your spirit lingers still.

We know where you've gone now is only a

part of God's great will.

We know if we live this life right,

we shall live again.

We'll see you on the other side

our father and our friend.

You Just Held On

When life stopped and threw you a curve,
you didn't step aside nor did you swerve.

You just held on...

When the doctor walked in
and shook his head,
you didn't say a word,
you just went to your bed.

You just held on...

When the angels came and rescued you,
you didn't become distraught
for they were coming for you.

You just held on...

Now you're rocking in the arms
of Jesus' love.
You're singing with the angels
in heaven above.
That is your reward for holding on...
So the rest of us
just have to be strong.
Keep the faith and restrain from all sin.
Until the Lord calls us home,
where we shall see you again.

Sister-N-Law

To think that you're gone
just seems like it can't be true.
No matter how we acted up,
you knew we loved you
A sister-n-law, who was more like a sis.
Your very presence, your smile,
your sense of humor,
all of that we're going to miss.
You had all of
the information, motivation, and
encouragement we needed.
To know that you're gone,
our hearts will surely grieve.
We thank God for the time
He loaned you to us.
We know we'll see you again
if it's in God we trust.

Mom

I don't know where to begin
I don't know where to start.
The day you left, really broke my heart.
The pain is present, it's here right now.
I'm trusting God to make it somehow.
If heaven had a phone,
I'd call you everyday
and these are the words that I would say.

Mom, I loved you in life.
In death, I love you more.
One sweet day we will walk
together on that Heavenly shore.
A million times I'll miss your smile.
A billion times I'll miss your face.
I know for certain you're the one person
I could never, ever, replace.

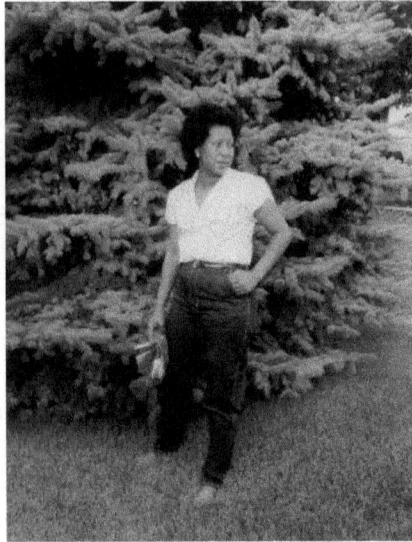

Nobody Knows

Nobody knows the pain I felt

when God called you home.

The room was full, yet I felt all alone.

You're the one person that has been

with me all my life.

Like a sister or brother

or maybe someone's wife.

You showed me how to walk,

talk and how to give God all the praise.

That's why I'll miss you
the balance of my days.
Nobody knows of the hole in my heart.
All I can do is pray and
wait for God to do His part.
The Word says He won't put more on you
than you can bear.
Well God, I truly have had my share.
Yet I know you won't leave me
nor forsake me.
But God, I'm just crying out
because I need Thee.
Nobody knows about this pain.
I'm sure it will be here for a while.
But for you God, I'll bear it and
face the world with a smile.

My Dad My Friend

You were the one who said to me
when I was just a boy,
follow me as I follow God.
That's what made this day so very hard.
You started out a father,
then became my friend.
Our relationship stayed strong
until the very end.
Dad, I'm gone miss you more
than you will ever know.
You embellished my life.
You helped me to grow
to the father I am today.
These memories in my heart and
head they'll stay.
A father, a solider, a motivator too.
Only God knows how much I'll miss you.
So long dad, I know I'll see you again.

Thanks always for being my dad
and my friend.

Brother From Another Mother

My brother from another mother.

That's what we called each other.

Cutting school, chasing girls and

just having fun.

Thinking you were the big guy 'cause you

were first to have a son.

All the things we did just being young.

This has shocked me and

took me for a loop.

It was just last week when we shot hoops.

They say death will come

in the twinkling of an eye.

But not once did I think

that my buddy would die.

These tears I'm crying are so sincere.

Because God knows

I wish my brother was here.

My Son

Every young man dreams of
one day having a son.
To mold them and make them
the man they have become.
I had this son, my lil' mini-me.
The grasp of death just stole you from me.
I tell you I'm left with
this giant hole in my heart.
Searching for words
there's no stop or a start.
I'm dumbfounded. I'm lost.
I hope it's a dream.
Every time I think about it,
I just wanna scream.
Looking to God for guidance and grace.
This is the one day I never wanted to face.
Good-bye my son, that's just for now.
I'm praying to God I'll make it somehow.

Like Father like Son

That's the phrase I would
always hear people say
when they saw us together
nearly every day.
I really don't know, nor do I have a clue,
what my life will be like without you.
I watched you grow from a boy to a man.
Losing you, I know, was the Master's plan.
It seems like just yesterday I was teaching
you to talk, walk and catch a ball.
Now you're adhering,
to the Master's great call.
My spirits are down.
My head is hanging low.
You will still be with me in my heart
no matter where I go.

Hallelujah

My soul cries out hallelujah

for all you brought me through.

I know without you,

I don't know what I would do.

I've had some ups and
you know I've had some downs.
Every time I wanted to quit, you were
somewhere around.
My soul shouts hallelujah.
I'm so full of joy. I just feel so free.
And it all comes because
I got down on my knees.
Thanking Him in advance for blessings
yet to come.
For blessing me with the time
I shared with Dad and Mom,
and all my other loved ones
that He called home.
For I know right now in heaven they roam.
Thank you Father!
All my praise belongs to you.
And from the depths of my heart,
I will always love you.

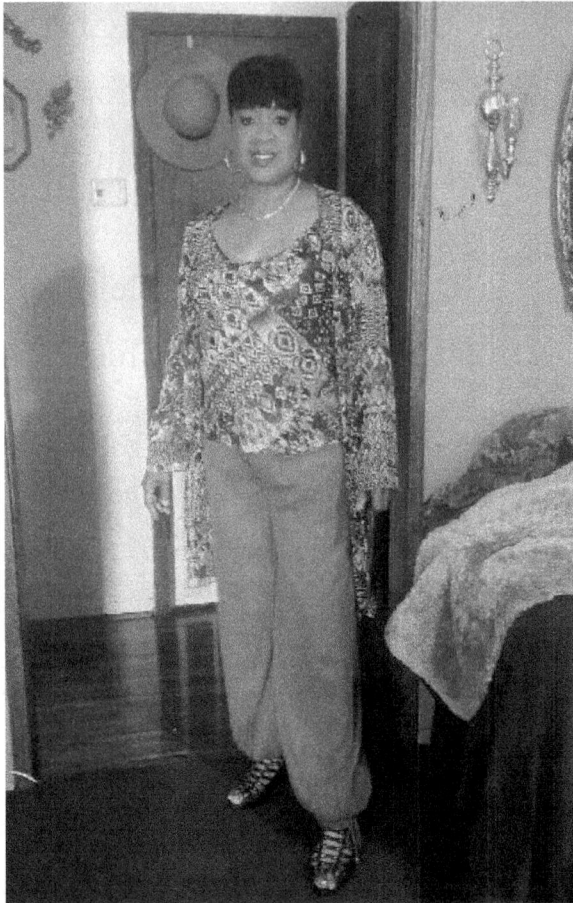

He Gave Me One More Day

I woke up this morning and shouted,

"Thank You!"

I got another chance to tell him,

"GOD I Love You."

One more day to do

what I didn't do the day before.

To help someone in need,

to love a little more.

For God loves us in spite of all our wrongs.

He advises to try again and

try to be strong.

We face trials each and every day.

The answer is get on your knees and

pray, pray, and pray.

But you can look at life just like this.

Things don't always work out

the way you wish.

Keep striving, trying, falling and getting

back up again.

Praying for another day and showing

yourself as a friend.

Don't Ever Give Up

Life takes you on a ride.

You go up hill and down.

Sometimes you'll land flat on the ground.

Body bruised and bumped and

a dent here and there.

The answer to this mystery,

go to God in prayer.

He'll lead you back right

where life dropped you off.

You'll stumble, shake your head,

and maybe even cough.

But don't you give up and don't give in.

'Cause in God, always,

you got a good friend.

When trials come your way and

be sure they will,

go down on your knees.

His compassion you will feel.

He's got all the answers

if you listen close for a few,

because this is for certain,

God truly loves you.

His Name is Prez

You came to us when our church
had all but fallen apart.
You rushed right in and
stole all our hearts.
You gave us the words that
He had given you.
Sometimes hard to swallow,
but yet all true.
You showed us you were human and had
been knocked down a time or two.
And strangers come from everywhere
wanting to know who you are.
His name is Prez, Pastor Jackson to you.
A man of God both tested and true.
This man does not brag nor does he boast.
But his works tell the story
he has really done the most.
The children he adores and

wishes and prays for the best.

The elderly he befriends

way more than the rest.

He loves all his flock and they love him too.

'Cause Prez (Pastor Jackson), is tried,

tested and true.

Still Standing

After all the trials and
tribulations I've been
through,
I looked to the hills that's
where I would see you.
The race is not given to
the swift, but those who
endure to the end.
You have shown yourself
a comforter and a friend.
I'm still standing. My loved ones are gone.
I'm still standing though life has all but
knocked me down.
I'm still standing though my face
sometimes has a frown.
I'm still standing
'cause you are on the throne.
O God I thank you!! I praise you too.

Because if it weren't for you,

what would I do?

I'm still standing and

I give you all the praise.

And all the praise is what

I'll give you for the rest of my days.

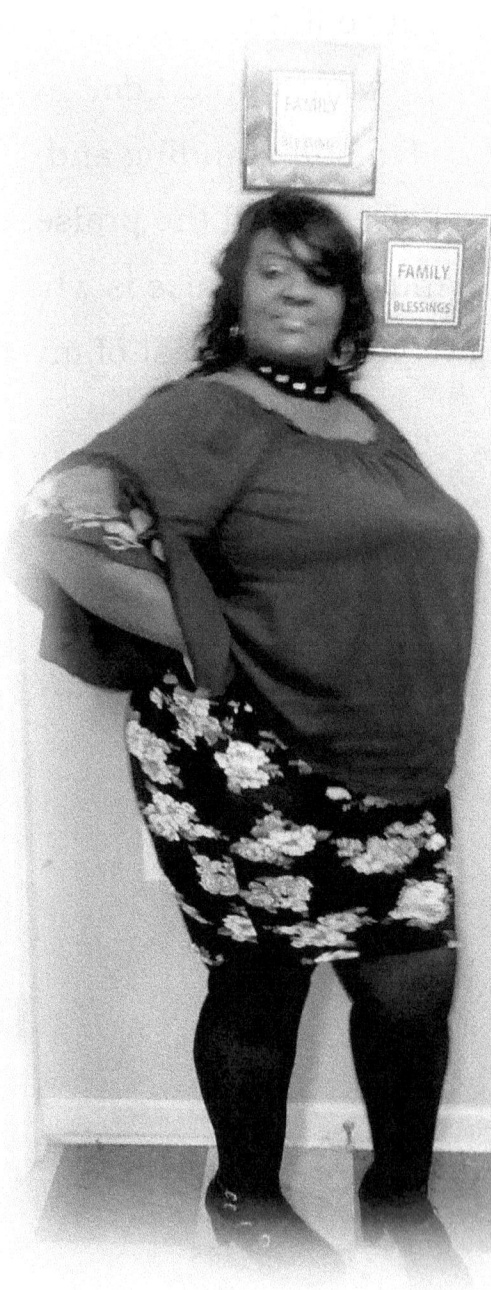

About the Author

Shirley Stokes was born in the small town of Crenshaw, MS to the union of Flynn and Velma Stokes in a Christian home. Later in life she reared her own family, which consisted of 3 sons and 3 daughters.

Her love of poetry started at a young age, but diminished slightly as she had her hands full raising her family. In 2000, after losing both parents and numerous other family members, she began to write again. Then, in 2013, after the untimely demise of her own daughter Raashad, she felt compelled to write this book of poetry. For Shirley, poetry let her escape the grief and at the same time show gratitude to God for being ever-present during all the grief.

www.ingramcontent.com/pod-product-compliance
Lightning Source LLC
Chambersburg PA
CBHW071642050426
42443CB00026B/942